T0329004

PRAISE FOR ROBERT LEE BREWER'S POETRY PROMPTS

"I have stacks of books on my desk, by my bed, and piled in my office. Some have been there for months. This book arrived, I opened it, and I immediately took it into my Poetry Workshop the next day … and the day after that … and the day after that …" —Joe Mills, author of *Exit, Pursued by a Bear*

"Robert Lee Brewer's prompts reached me at time when, after twenty years of writing, I was becoming disillusioned with the art form. The gentle and copious inspirational offers he gave reinvigorated my creative practice, and I've continued to write, publish, perform, and teach poetry ever since." —Daniel Ari, Richmond, California poet laureate and author of *One Way to Ask*

"Robert Lee Brewer's prompts stopped me staring aimlessly at a blank page and helped focus my writing in directions I would never have otherwise gone." —Tracy Davidson

"Robert Lee Brewer's poetry prompts are tiny sparks of ideas that make their way into much of my poetry. They've been a constant catalyst for my poems being published in journals like *Rattle* and *The Adirondack Review*, and I go to them daily for their inspiration …" —Richard Fenwick, author of *Unusual Sorrows*

"After teaching about poetry and writing for years, I started taking my own poetry-writing seriously beginning with Robert Lee Brewer's regular prompts. They are specific enough to get my wheels turning, while allowing enough flexibility to interpret them as I choose." —Nancy Posey, author of *Let the Lady Speak*

"Robert's prompts have brought good results for me. In fact, many poems from my upcoming chapbook resulted from his prompts." —Nancy Breen, author of *Burying the Alleluia*, a Top 10 finalist for the New Women's Voices award

"A few years ago, at a time when my writing was withering from the pressures of my work life, I discovered Robert Lee Brewer's April PAD Challenge, where he provided daily prompts for writing poems. These I embraced with fervor and since then I have been hooked on his poetry prompts, which have revitalized my writing." —Lelawattee Manoo-Rahming

"Many of my published poems—and at least one chapbook—are the direct result of Robert's inspiring prompts. They're the perfect jump-start for a recalcitrant muse." —Bruce W. Niedt, author of *Breathing Out*

"Robert's poetry prompts were the keys which unlocked the rusty door of my creative mind and helped me rediscover my love of writing poetry back in 2008. I just had to blow off the cobwebs and turn on the lights." —Michelle Hed

"The first time I met Robert in person was at a poetry festival, and shortly after that I became even more excited about his creativity, humor, and diligence, as I immersed myself in the poeming process at his Poetic Asides website. He also impresses me as one of the best teachers anywhere. Ever. Period." —gpr crane

"Like a good question challenges my perceptions, Robert Lee Brewer's prompts nudge me in new directions, help me apply a new angle of vision to an old idea, or dare me to discover possibilities. Those prompts are catalysts for growing as a writer because they keep me thinking and moving toward greater understanding of often misplaced experiences." —Jane Shlensky, author of *Barefoot on Gravel*

"I tend to write poetry out of what's happening in my life at the time. Robert Lee Brewer's prompts always inspire me to look at my life with fresh eyes." —julie l. elder

"A poet's unique perspective may be unleashed by a single word or idea. Prompts from Robert Lee Brewer free writers to explore remote nooks and crannies resulting in poetic treasures as varied as the genre itself." —Pat Anthony

"Robert Lee Brewer's creative poetry prompts have enriched my life. His prompts are alluring invitations that inspire me to delve inward, reflect through a poetic lens, and hone my poetic voice. Much to my delight, several of the prompt-based poems got published and some won awards in poetry writing contests." —Dr. Nurit Israeli

"Robert Lee Brewer's poetry prompts placed me on a path of daily writing, and communicating with poets that leave me in awe. That was April 2009. Enough said." —Marie Elena Good

"The prompts and challenges provided by Robert Lee Brewer on the Poetic Asides website have been an amazing inspiration for me. His thoughtful themes have provided a framework and a creative starting point for some of my most interesting and fun poems. Additionally, his site has fostered and encouraged one of the most supportive communities of poets I've ever known." —RJ Clarken, author of *Mugging for the Camera*

"Inspiration can strike out of the blue, but sometimes it needs a little nudge. Robert Lee Brewer's poetry prompts are perfect for drawing poems out of you that you didn't even know were there." —Nikki Markle

"I had given up on poetry, thinking a writer begins with something to say, and I had no important ideas. Following (and fighting) prompts, I discover that there's more within than even I knew from the surface." —Barbara E. Young

"Robert Lee Brewer's prompts throw me curves—unexpected ideas that encourage me to write. They improve my poetic batting average." —William Preston

SMASH POETRY JOURNAL

125 Writing Ideas for Inspiration and Self-Exploration

Robert Lee Brewer

An imprint of Penguin Random House LLC
penguinrandomhouse.com

ISBN 978-1-4403-0061-5

Edited by Amy Jones
Designed by Jason Williams

146119709

DEDICATION

For all the poets, whether they know it or not.

ACKNOWLEDGMENTS

This book wouldn't exist without all the poets who have poemed along with me at the Poetic Asides blog for more than a decade now. All the poems that spring from each prompt still surprise and delight me. Thank you, all!

In a more direct and specific way, I want to thank Pam Wissman for suggesting this project in the first place. Also, I'm indebted to the great care of my editor, Amy Jones, as well as the killer design—inside and out—of Jason Williams. Y'all totally nailed it!

Finally, I want to thank my wife, Tammy, who has been here since the beginning, encouraging me when I didn't know what to expect and supporting me through the thick and thin ever since. She really is my compass at times.

Of course, there are others to thank (didn't forget you, Mom), but only so much space. If you're wondering if I'm thinking of you, there's a very good chance that I am. Thank you!

INTRODUCTION

Let's start at the beginning.

It was March 2008 when I got an idea for my relatively new blog, Poetic Asides, on the WritersDigest.com website. After months of posting about various poetry-related topics, I wanted to try and get more interaction with my readers (if I even had any).

The idea was simple: Post a poetry prompt each day of April—also known as National Poetry Month—and encourage people to post their poems in the comments. I'd share my own attempt at a poem along with the prompt to get people started. But there was a small problem.

As with any new project, I had absolutely no idea how people would respond. In fact, I didn't know if anyone would respond at all. Comments on my blog posts were few and far between.

I still remember the evening of March 31, 2008, like it was yesterday.

Talking on the phone to the person who would become my wife in only four months time, I said, "I've got this poem-a-day challenge I'm going to try out tomorrow morning. It should be a fun challenge, but I don't know if anyone is going to participate besides maybe one or two people. There's a chance it may just be me."

On the next day, I was shocked to find out it wasn't just me, and it wasn't just one or two people. That first poetry prompt, which was to write a poem about a first or a series of firsts, eventually received nearly 300 comments.

And the April Poem-a-Day (PAD) Challenge was born. It was so popular that I kept the poeming going weekly after the month was over with the Wednesday Poetry Prompts, which are still going strong (458 prompts and counting as of this writing). In November of the same year, I started the first ever November Poem-a-Day Chapbook Challenge—with a goal of poeming each day of November and collecting the poems into a chapbook manuscript during the month of December.

All told, I've now shared more than 1,000 poetry prompts and example poems on my Poetic Asides blog, and I have no plans of ending that run. Partly, because it keeps me writing, and writing keeps me sane. If I don't write at any other time, I know I will write a poem each Wednesday for the blog—and that's enough to keep me from going dark or drying up completely.

Another reason I keep going is that I hear from people every year who broke their silence as a result of the prompts. People who write their first ever poems. Poets who break out of ruts in their writing—sometimes ruts that had lasted years (even decades). Poets who find a new community of other poets from around the country and the world. Even teachers who use the prompts to inspire their students to write poems.

I like to think of it as the power of the prompt, and even I didn't realize the depth of this power in the beginning. One thing I've learned first hand is that one simple prompt can turn into more than 1,000 unique poems from more than 1,000 poets. Then, the next prompt can turn into another 1,000 poems. And so on.

You're currently holding that power in your hands. But make no mistake: These prompts are powerless without you and your willingness to dive in and take the risk of writing that first line. It doesn't need to be perfect. It doesn't even need to be poetic. You see, that's how first drafts work.

Just write. Write what springs into your mind. Sketch ideas, images, incomplete phrases. Doodle, if you must. But I've found that breaking the safety of all that white space is the best way to get closer to my poem. And I know that anyone can do it. Even if you've never written a poem before, you can do this. If you're not feeling the first prompt, jump to the second prompt or the tenth prompt or the last prompt. Flip to a random page and just start writing.

Once you've written that first poem, you'll be hungry to write the next poem. Another thing I've learned is that poems beget poems. It won't be long until you can't turn the poetry off, and that's a wonderful feeling.

After you've written those first drafts, you may feel the impulse to revise them—or recreate them, which is my preferred terminology. Eventually, you may even try to get them published.

But all of that is secondary. Before you can recreate poems or get them published, one thing needs to happen: Just write.

I believe in you, and I hope someday you'll share what you've written.

Until that day comes, keep poeming!

—Robert Lee Brewer

1

GRAND OPENING

Write an "open" poem. The poem could be about physically opening something: a garage door, a bottle of soda, or your mouth. The poem could also go the metaphorical route of opening a can of worms or Pandora's box. Or if you're into golf or tennis, write about the U.S., French, or British Opens. It's all open to interpretation.

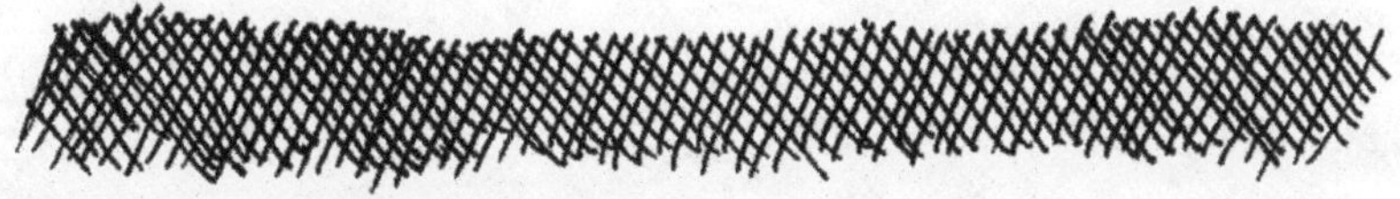

THE ART POETIC

Write an ekphrastic poem. That is, a poem based on a piece of visual art—a painting, a photograph, a sculpture. Your choice.

WHAT IS AN EKPHRASTIC POEM?

An ekphrastic poem is one filled with imagery of a scene or a work of art including sculptures, paintings, drawings, architecture, and yes, portraits. In addition to imagery, the poem may critique, imitate, dramatize, or reflect upon the artwork.

3

SENSORY LIES

Write a "senses" poem. That is, write a poem that uses one or more of your senses. Smell, taste, touch, sound, sight, or even a sixth sense. Focus on one of them or try to incorporate them all.

INSECTUM

Make an insect the title of your poem, and then, write your poem. Possible titles include: "Praying Mantis," "Ants," and "Grasshoppers." Or incorporate other creepy crawlies, like spiders, slugs, and leeches (shiver). Sorry in advance if this prompt gives you the heebie-jeebies; feel free to use insect repellent in your verse.

5

I AM A POEM

Write a "metaphor" poem. That is, write a poem built around a metaphor. Remember: Metaphors actually take on another object (like "I am a Tree" or "I am a Rock"). This is not to be confused with similes, which are like metaphors (for instance, "I am like a tree" or "I am like a rock"), but not quite. Dig? If so, then you are a shovel or spade or bulldozer. Now poem the heck out of your metaphors.

STRANGER DANGER

Write a "danger" poem. There are various levels of danger out there—from physical danger to the danger of being discovered doing something you shouldn't (or doing something that might embarrass you—or someone else). Even the act of writing and sharing a poem brings with it the potential for danger.

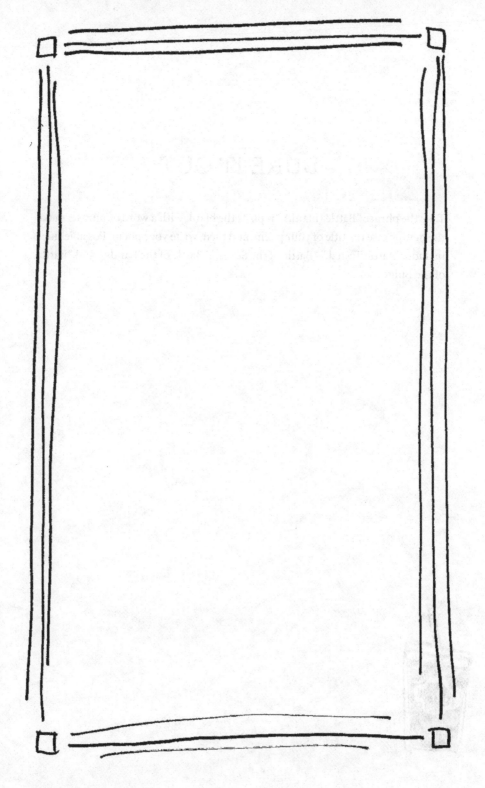

7

DUKE IT OUT

Take the phrase "Battle (blank)," replace the blank with a word or phrase, make the new phrase the title of your poem, and then, write your poem. Possible titles include: "Battle Tested," "Battle of the Sexes," "Battle of the Bands," and "Battle of the Bulge."

COMPETITIVE POETRY

Believe it or not, poetry can be a competitive sport. In fact, that's a big part of the popularity for slam poetry. Slam is a form of performance poetry in which poets perform a poem (usually three minutes or less) and receive scores—kind of like *America's Got Talent* or *American Idol*, but with poetry. But it's not set up to be stressful. Rather, it's about celebrating great performances!

SUPER STAR

Write a "super" poem. Fans of sports, advertising, and half-time shows may think of the Super Bowl. Comics and movie fans know all about superheroes *and* super villains. Folks familiar with quarter machines surely are acquainted with the super ball (a bouncy little sphere of endless amusement). But whatever your definition of super, this is a great opportunity to write a super poem.

PASSWORD PROTECTED

Write a "password" poem. Write about someone using passwords, creating a password, or you could hide a password (or words) in your poem (perhaps, à la an acrostic poem). Have fun with it.

WHAT IS AN ACROSTIC POEM?

An acrostic poem is when the first letter of each line spells out a word or phrase, adding extra meaning to your verse. Double acrostics spell words with the first and last letter of each line. Meanwhile, telestich is the term used when you spell words only using the final letter of each line. So there are plenty of hidden message possibilities!

ELEVATION STATION

Write an "elevated" poem. Whether we're talking elevators, elevator shoes, elevating for a slam dunk, or some other form of elevation, there's really only one way to take this prompt: Up! That is, unless you want to share the aftermath of elevation, which is often down.

11

PIN UP

Write a "bulletin board" poem. Or maybe a more modern version of this is the eraser board poem. In other words, write a poem that might be tacked onto a bulletin board or scribbled on an eraser board or even magnetized to a refrigerator. Probably something short, something personal, maybe even timely.

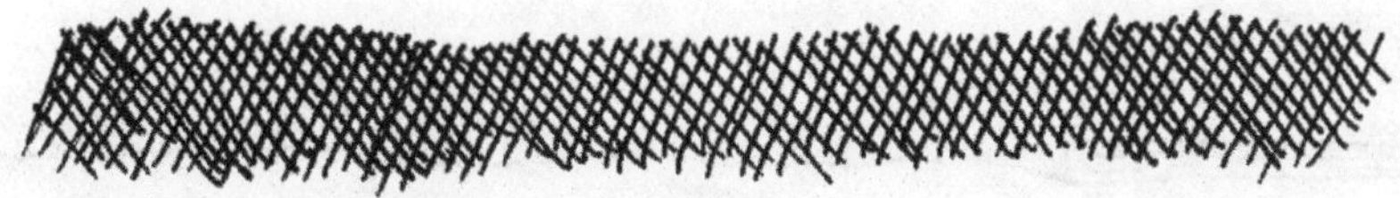

12

HOME AWAY FROM HOME

Write a "second home" poem. Most people have a first home—even if it's just the place where you lay your head or stash your heart. But many people also have a second home—a place that is like a home away from home. Write a poem about such a place.

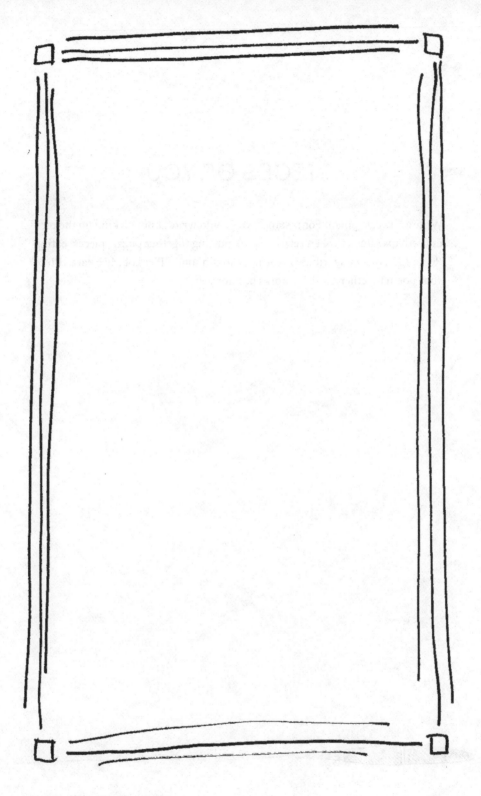

13

PIECES OF YOU

Write a "pieces" poem. For instance, you could write about picking up the pieces (perhaps after a broken relationship), putting together puzzle pieces, eating Reese's Pieces, or pay tribute to the Janis Joplin song, "Piece of My Heart." Piece your poem together however works best for you.

14

INTROSPECTION REFLECTION

Take the phrase "I am a (blank)," replace the blank with a word or phrase, make the new phrase the title of your poem, and then, write your poem. Possible titles could include: "I Am a Toothbrush," "I Am a Martian," or "I Am a Replica X-Wing Fighter."

15

ONE MORE POEM

Write a "plus one" poem. It could be a math poem. Or a poem about including a guest (or "plus one"). Or a poem about doing something just "one more time." Or the new person in a group, new task at work, and so on and so forth.

DON'T FIB

Or actually, do fib. The fib is a rare mathematical poetic form that follows the Fibonacci sequence for syllable count in each line. That is, the first and second lines have one syllable each; the third line has two syllables; fourth line three syllables; and fifth line contains five syllables. If you kept it up for 10 lines, you'd have a 55-syllable line of poetry. Woah!

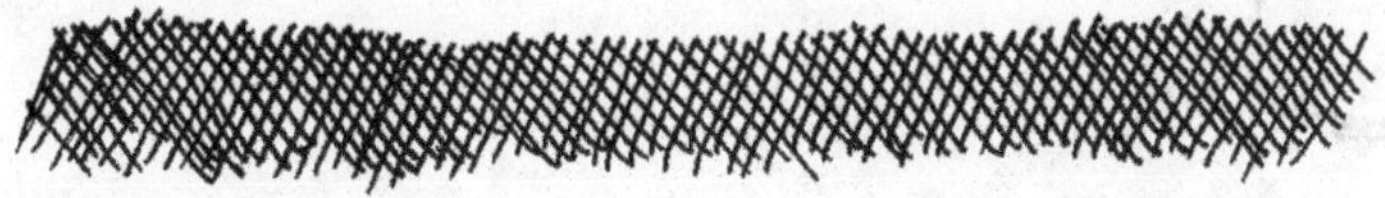

16

GREATER THAN

Write a "bigger" poem. Have you been to Texas? Everything's supposed to be bigger in Texas, right? Sometimes even smaller things (like our sun compared to other suns) are also bigger things (like our sun compared to the planets in our solar system). Write bigger!

17

SOME ASSEMBLY REQUIRED

Write an "assembly" poem. An assembly poem could be about a meeting (an assembly of people). Or an assembly poem could be about an assembly line or assembling something or whatever else you can assemble with your poetic mind.

QUICK PICK UP

Write a "napkin" poem. It could be a poem about a napkin or that involves napkins, but the thought for this kind of poem would be a poem that might be scrawled onto a napkin in a rush—or maybe even slipped across (or under) the table to someone sitting with you. So maybe a warning or an invitation.

19

DOODLY-DO

Write a "doodle" poem. This could start off as something small that stays small or builds to epic proportions. Doodle around a bit and see what develops. If needed, start by describing something close at hand or within your current field of vision.

TRY THIS

Consider making your short doodle poem a *cobla*, or a poem that is just a single stanza long.

THAT'S A NEGATIVE

Write a "nope" poem. A nope poem, I suppose, could be about saying no to a certain situation, person, or thing. Like saying nope to live concerts, people who like debating everything, or mushrooms.

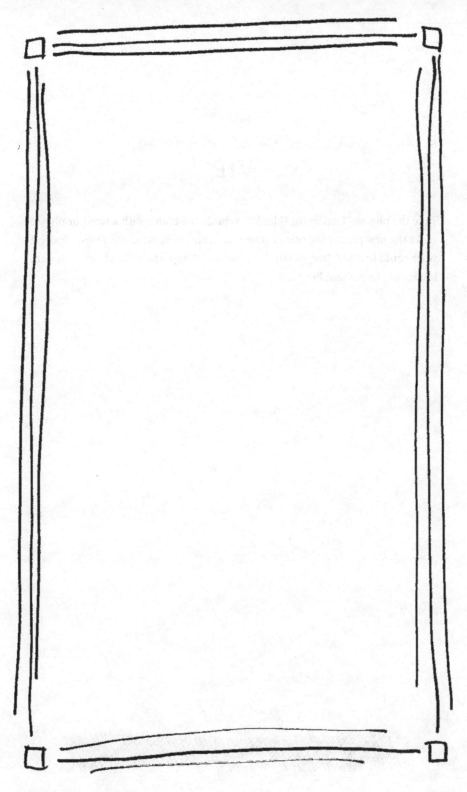

21

VIP

Take the phrase "Important (blank)," replace the blank with a word or phrase, make the new phrase the title of your poem, and then, write the poem. Possible titles could include: "Important Documents," "Important: Read Before Assembling," or "Important People."

SAVE YOURSELF

Write a "selfish" poem. We can also consider this the Ebenezer Scrooge poem (pre-ghosts).

THREE-LINERS

Did you know that three-line stanzas are called tercets? Or that there are three-line poems that are not called haiku? It's true! Other three-liners include the senryu (which is what most people write when they think they're writing haiku), sijo, kimo, katauta, lune, and hay(na)ku. Plus, there's a form called tricube that consists of three stanzas with three lines and three syllables in each line. What a trifecta!

23

TALK ABOUT THE WEATHER

Write an "under the weather" poem. You can use the turn of speech, which means sick or not feeling good. Or you could be literal and actually be under the weather, whether that's good or not.

THIS MONTH

Pick a month (any month), make it the title of your poem, and then, write your poem. Possible months include January, February, March, (cruel) April, May, June, or even July, August, September, October, November, or December. Yes, there are twelve possible months; choose well, or write twelve poems.

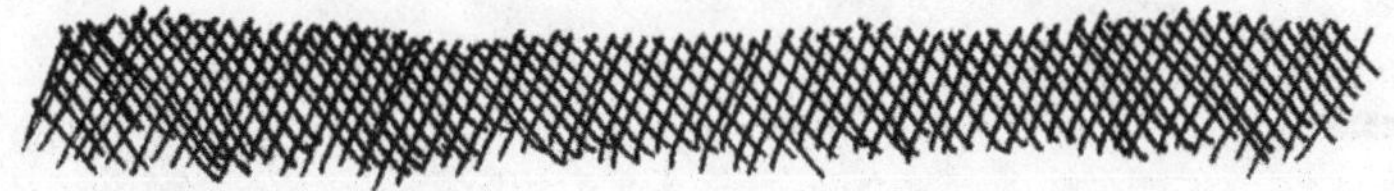

25

HIDE AND SEEK

Write a "hiding" poem. The poem could be about someone hiding or something hidden. Or the process of searching. And remember: There are physical things that can hide, but also thoughts, emotions, plans, and so much more.

TRY THIS

Confessional poetry shares personal, private, or other secretive details, usually about religion or emotions. Maybe your hiding poem turned into a confessional poem!

26

CAN'T HARDLY WAIT

Write an "anticipation" poem. A person could anticipate an early spring or a lover's fling; a person could anticipate any old thing.

FRAMED

Write a "portrait" poem. You can use an actual portrait to write an ekphrastic poem. Or think up an image from real life. Or fake life. Or don't be so literal; instead of writing a poem that describes a portrait, use the poem to frame a moment or lifestyle or whatever. By the way, how many times did I type "or" in this paragraph?

STAR POWER

Take the phrase "Star (blank)," replace the blank with a word or phrase, make the new phrase the title of your poem, and then, write the poem. Possible titles include: "Star-struck," "Star Man," "Star Wars Prequels Aren't Star Wars Movies," "Starter Set," or "Stark Raving Mad."

ERASURE POEMS

One way to create by deleting is through the process of "writing" erasure poems. Also known as blackout poetry, erasure poetry is the process of taking a piece of text—like a newspaper article or website post—and deleting the original text until you're left with a new poem. When I turned thirty-seven, I hacked away at Walt Whitman's epic poem "Song of Myself" to create my own song. Fun exercise.

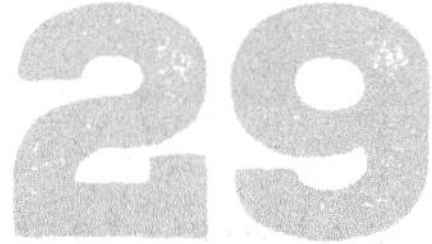

DISBELIEF

Write an "it can't be" poem. That is, a poem about something that just can't be true. For some, this might mean a heart-broken love poem at the end of a relationship. For others, it might be dealing with a death. Still, it could be as trivial as a sports team losing or running out of chocolate (gasp!).

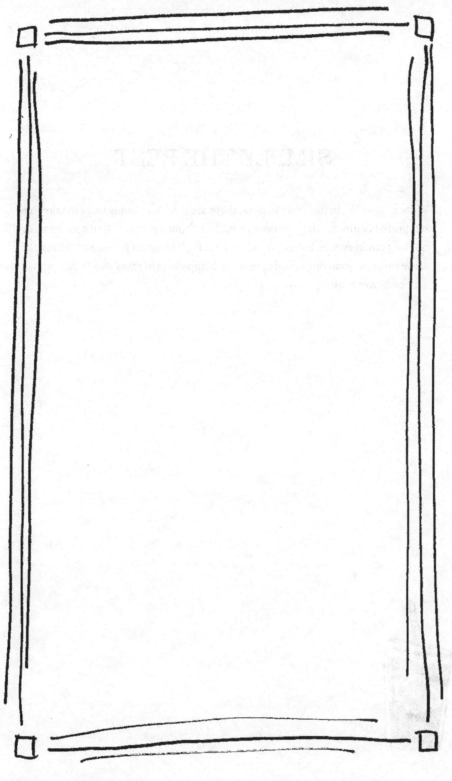

30

SIMPLY THE BEST

Write a "nothing better" poem. Now, there are at least a couple ways to take this, but probably more. First, the poem could be about a moment that's so amazing nothing could ever be better—kind of like a high moment poem. But taking the same prompt, someone could spin it the complete other way as a "nothing will ever be better again" poem.

31

DREAMING IS FREE

Write a “dream” poem. So many things happen in our dreams—or, at least, in my dreams. Of course, if you don’t have dreams, then write a poem about a dream job, dream relationship, dream vacation, or some other dream situation.

DREAM POEMS

I love writing dream poems. In fact, my *Solving the World's Problems* collection of poems has not one, but two poems titled "dream." But there are many other great dream poems you can check out as well. Here are a few:

- "Dream Variations" by Langston Hughes
- "Echo" by Christina Rossetti
- "Imitation" by Edgar Allan Poe
- "Dreaming the Breasts" by Anne Sexton
- "The Sleepers" by Walt Whitman
- "I Dreamed I Wrote This Sestina Wearing My Maidenform Bra" by Denise Duhamel

32

TAPERED EFFECT

Write a "tape" poem. The poem could be about transparent tape, duct tape, video tape, or even tapeworm. Anything that you can bend into a tape poem is fair game.

33

IMITATION GAME

Write an "imitation" poem. Some folks say imitation is the best form of flattery. Find a poem by another poet and imitate his or her style, subject matter, or tone.

POEMS TO IMITATE

Not sure where to start when it comes to finding poems to imitate? No problem. Here are some popular poems you can find with a quick online search:

- "Aubade With Burning City" by Ocean Vuong
- "Good Bones" by Maggie Smith
- "This Is Just to Say" by William Carlos Williams
- "The Translator" by Sandra Beasley
- "One man band" by Bob Hicok

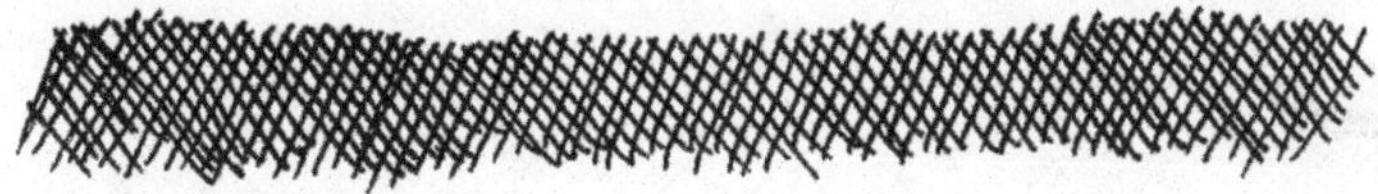

34

SHARING IS CARING

Write a "sharing" poem. A poem about somebody sharing something. Or a poem about receiving something that was shared. Or witnessing an act of sharing. Or . . .

35

THREE FOR THEE

Take the phrase "Three (blank)," replace the blank with a word or phrase, make the new phrase the title of your poem, and then, write your poem. Possible titles include: "Three Blind Hippos," "Three Muskrats," "Three's Company," or "Three Movies Is Too Many for The Hobbit, Peter Jackson (just saying)."

POPULARITY CONTEST

Pick a popular saying, make it the title of your poem, and then, write your poem. Possible titles might include: "May the Force Be With You," "It's a Bird; It's a Plane; It's Superman," "Just Do It," or "Break a Leg."

37

COMMON GROUND

Write a poem about a commonplace location. The poem could be about the local grocery store, library, or something even more intimate—like your kitchen or bathroom. Or it could be standing in line at the DMV or post office.

POEMS OF PLACE

Place has always been an important element of poetry from Dante's *Inferno* to Chaucer's *The Canterbury Tales*. Here are a few poems in which place plays a major role:

- "Stopping by Woods on a Snowy Evening" by Robert Frost
- "We Real Cool" by Gwendolyn Brooks
- "The Apple Trees at Olema" by Robert Hass
- "Going Home" by Wislawa Szymborska
- "Graveyard Blues" by Natasha Trethewey

38

PAPER LINES

Write a "paper" poem. The poem could be about something made of paper, made with paper, or a document—like a contract, deed, will, etc. It's a great chance to unpack your origami poems, paper plane poems, or even your spit ball poems. Maybe you can even write it on paper.

39

ROLLING, ROLLING, ROLLING

Write a "let the good times roll" poem. Focus on the "good times" or play around with the concept of "rolling."

40

YOU'RE A NATURAL

Write a "natural" poem. A poem about something natural. It could be a natural way of living, something made of natural materials, nature itself, or some other spin.

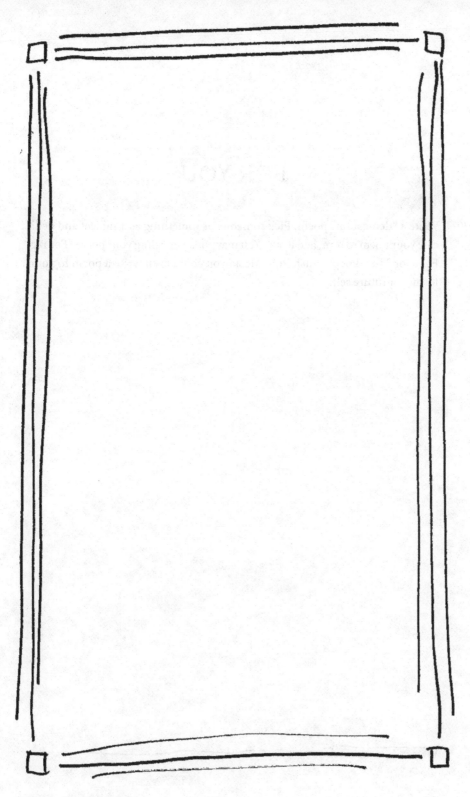

41

FOR YOU

Write a "dedication" poem. Pick someone or something as a subject and dedicate your poem to him, her, it, etc. You may consider titling your poem "For Big Foot" or "To a Purple Push Pin." Heck, you could even write a poem to your former or future self.

ON ODES

In contemporary poetry, odes are most commonly poems that pay direct tribute to a person, place, or thing. Often, they are straightforward praise poems, but some poets employ wit and irony in their odes, because what would poetry be without a little rule-bending and/or -breaking, right?

42

LET ME COUNT THE WAYS

Take the phrase "(blank) Ways to (blank)," replace the blanks with a word or phrase, make that the title of the poem, and then, write the poem. Possible titles could include: "The Proper Ways to Write Poetry," "10 Ways to Fall in Love," and/or "Wrong Ways to Toronto."

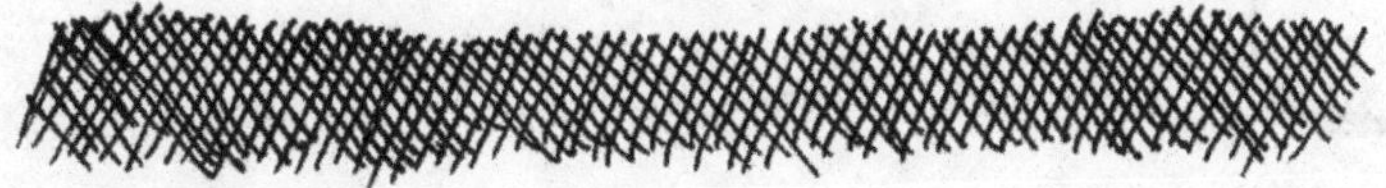

43

ONE OF A KIND

Write a "unique" poem. But aren't all poems unique? Like snowflakes, maybe they are. Write along the lines of unique situations, unique people, or unique (fill-in-the-blank). So while your poem may be unique, maybe it could cover something or someone unique. Feel free to put your unique spin on it.

JUST WRITE IT

Write an "activity" poem. Possible activities from which to choose: running, driving, folding clothes, tying knots, casting lines, dancing, sleeping, and so much more. Pick an activity and write it out.

FEAR

Write a "phobia" poem. There are so many possible phobias from which to choose, including some of the more popular phobias like arachnophobia (fear of spiders), claustrophobia (fear of confined spaces), acrophobia (fear of heights), and coulrophobia (fear of clowns).

46

HOUSE OF CARDS

Write a "card" poem. This poem could be a greeting card poem. But there are so many other varieties of cards, too, including business cards, credit cards, sports cards, playing cards, and the St. Louis Cards. When it comes to alcohol and tobacco, many folks get carded. Some people are referred to as being a card. And, well, there are many other possibilities in the cards.

47

WORTH THE STRUGGLE?

Write a "struggle" poem. Many people struggle with many things—work, finances, addiction, relationships, and even finding the time to write poems. But there are also cultural struggles, animal struggles, and even plant struggles. Pick a struggle and write a poem.

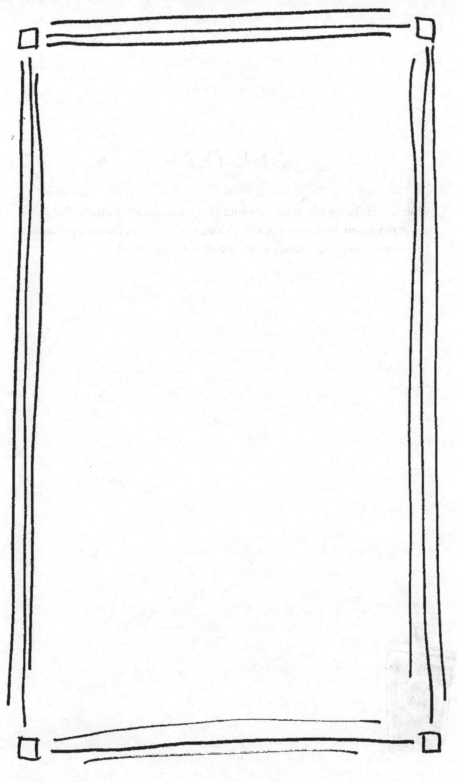

48

ONE YEAR

Write a "year in the life" poem. It could be a poem about something that takes a year to happen, a summary of a year's worth of events, or even a top moment. Poems about tree rings, seasons, etc., are all welcome as well.

CHILD'S PLAY

Take the phrase "Play (blank)," replace the blank with a word or phrase, make the new phrase the title of your poem, and then write the poem. Possible titles include: "Play Nice," "Play Fair," "Play Hard," or "Play the Guitar."

50

CONTROL ISSUES

Write an “uncontrollable” poem. There are so many daily things over which people feel they have no control: Politics, war, and drama are just a few. Some may rage against that feeling of helplessness; others may let themselves get pulled along by the current; but we can all write poems.

51

UTMOST IMPORTANCE

Write a "nothing important" poem. Maybe it's a poem about an unimportant tool, plant, animal, or even person. Of course, sometimes the unimportant things are revealed to be the most important of all. So leave no unimportant stone unturned in search of your poem.

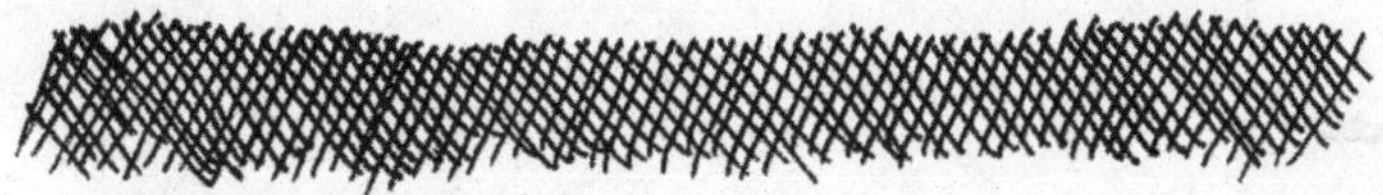

52

COORDINATED EFFORT

Write a "coordinated" poem. Coordination could refer to keeping your balance, but it can also be a coordinated event. Sports teams have coordinators; complicated processes require coordination; and even poems have to coordinate words, line breaks, and stanzas.

UNCOORDINATED POETRY

Believe it or not, there's actually a French poetic form that's basic premise is to be an uncoordinated, chaotic mess. The main rule of the descort is that the poem should not be the same from line to line or stanza to stanza. Varied syllable count, no end rhymes, no refrains, and unpredictability from one line to the next.

53

BOOKISH

Write a poem about a book. The book could be your favorite, or one that you loathe. The poem could literally be about the book, or maybe written in the voice of a character.

IN THE END

Write an "at last" poem. Or a "finally" poem. The poem could be about finally receiving a promotion, a proposal, a letter, an award, etc. Or it could be a poem about reaching a goal, like climbing a mountain or finishing your taxes.

55

IDENTIFYING FEATURE

Write a "persona" poem. In persona poems, poets write from the perspective of someone (or something) other than themselves. For instance, write a poem narrated by Ronda Rousey, Ron Burgundy, or a Bob Ross painting (yes, inanimate objects are fair game, too):

56

MAYBE?

Take the phrase "Call Me (blank)," replace the blank with a word or phrase, make the new phrase the title of your poem, and then write the poem. Possible titles include: "Call Me Al," "Call Me Crazy," "Call Me Batman," or "Call Me at 3 O'Clock in the Morning."

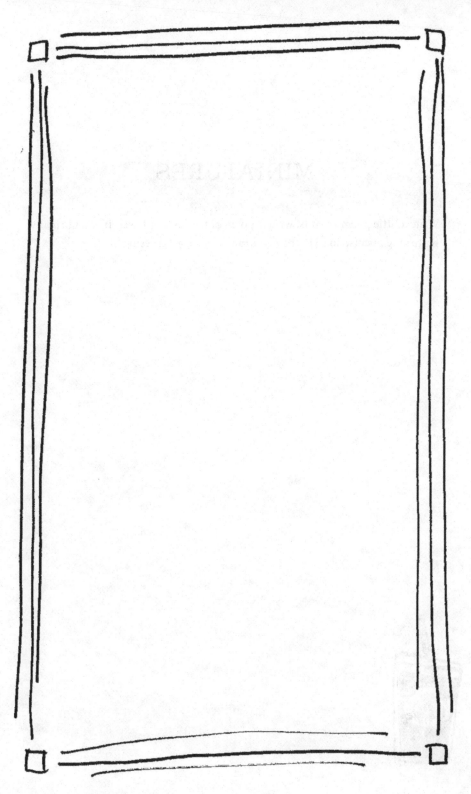

57

MINIATURES

Write a little poem. That is, write a poem of ten lines or fewer. If you normally write long poems, do so in the first draft. Then, start deleting lines.

POETIC FORMS OF TEN OR FEWER LINES

Earlier I mentioned several three-line poetic forms, but there are so many more at various lengths that are ten or fewer lines. Here are a few examples:

- Gwawdodyn—four lines
- Limerick—five lines
- Shadorma—six lines
- Rondelet—seven lines
- Triolet—eight lines
- Nonet—nine lines
- Dizain—ten lines

58

EYES WIDE OPEN

Write a "watching the world go by" poem. Whether you're watching from the window, a park bench, or a couch, perspective is one part of this prompt; the other is what one sees and thinks about it.

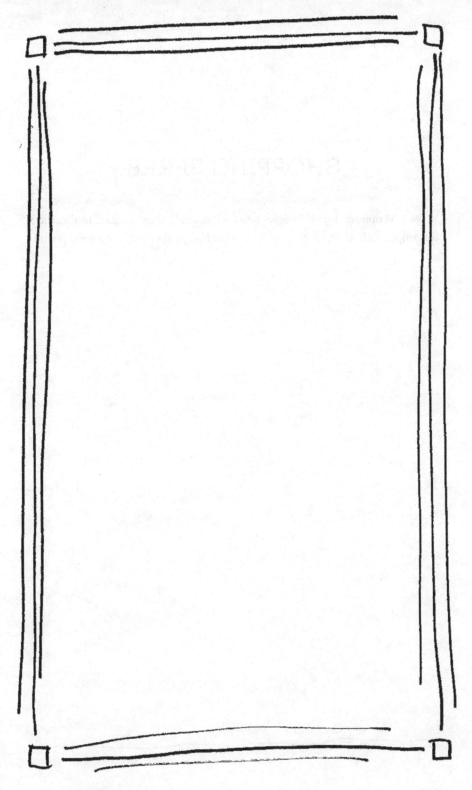

59

SHOPPING SPREE

Write a "shopping" poem. People shop for husbands, shop for good music, shop for people with similar interests, and so on. Happy shopping for a good poem!

60

CRAZY COMBOS

First, what is the color of the shirt you're currently wearing? (If you're not wearing a shirt, put one on before you catch a cold.) Second, think about the most recent animal you've seen (either in the wild, online, on TV, or in your imagination—this isn't rocket science). Now do a little math problem: (color of shirt I'm wearing) + (last animal I've seen) = (title of my poem). To get that title, combine the color of the shirt you're wearing with the last animal you've seen. Possible titles might be: "Turquoise Rabbit," "Crimson Blue Jay," or "Rainbow Hamster." If you prefer to change the color of your shirt or the selection of animal, go for it.

SPECTACULAR POEMING

Write a "spectacular" poem. Poems that are spectacular might be about BIG events or occurrences: Think Spectacular Spider-Man, or think about great spectacles (some good, some disastrous). Or look at the spectacular things that happen at an atomic or molecular level. Here's to spectacular poeming!

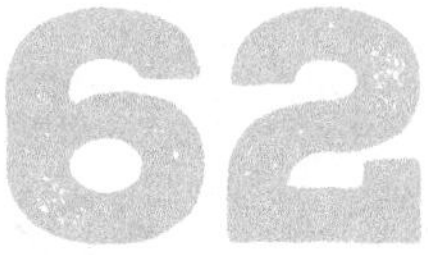

CARPE DIEM

Write a "hesitation" or "hesitant" poem. Aren't our lives filled with hesitations—large and small?

63

ON THE LOOKOUT

Take the phrase "Seeking (blank)," replace the blank with a word or phrase, make the new phrase the title of your poem, and then, write your poem. Possible titles might include: "Seeking Forgiveness," "Seeking Answers," "Seeking Peace, Love, & Understanding," and/or "Seeking an Original #27 Issue of *Detective Comics*."

ON DECK

Write a "next in line" poem. This could be a poem about somebody waiting in a line at the DMV or the grocery store, obviously. But it could also be about a line of lovers, a line of errors, or a line of poetry. What is coming up? What is around the corner? These could be topics for a "next in line" poem.

65

SHARING SECRETS

Write a "secret" poem. This poem can reveal a secret, incorporate a secret activity, or involve any other secret interpretation. It could be a poem written in code (acrostic, anyone?) or with double meanings.

THE GOLDEN SHOVEL

Terrance Hayes created this poetic form in his poem "The Golden Shovel" with a nod to Gwendolyn Brooks' "We Real Cool," which takes place at the Golden Shovel. The rules are simple: Take a line (or lines) from a poem you admire, use each word in the line (or lines) as an end word in your poem, and keep the end words in order. Of course, it's good form to give a nod to the original poet.

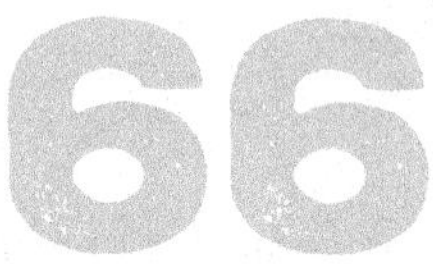

HIGH ALERT

Write an "alert" poem. People can be alert; they can alert others to situations; and, of course, they can put out an alert to whatever. Some alerts come with bells, whistles, and alarms; others are quiet. And alerts are not restricted to people; animals are often alert to the dangers and opportunities around them on a daily basis.

67

MORTAL INSTRUMENTS

Write a "dead" poem. The poem, of course, could be about a dead person, animal, or other formerly living creature. It could be about the undead or facing death. But then, there are things that die, too: computers, relationships, feelings. And some folks feel "dead to the world" or just "dead," though they are alive (it's an expression).

SHOUT IT OUT!

Think of something you might shout out loud (or hear others shout), make it the title of your poem, and then, write the poem. Possible titles include: "Way to Go," "Run for It," and "Fire" (though it's usually not good practice to scream "fire" without an actual fire).

69

CHA-CHA-CHA-CHANGES

Write a poem just as something changes or is about to change. This could mean big sweeping political or social changes, or it could mean when a candle is lit (or blown out), a room is entered, or an unexpected touch. Change can be exciting, scary, and, well, different.

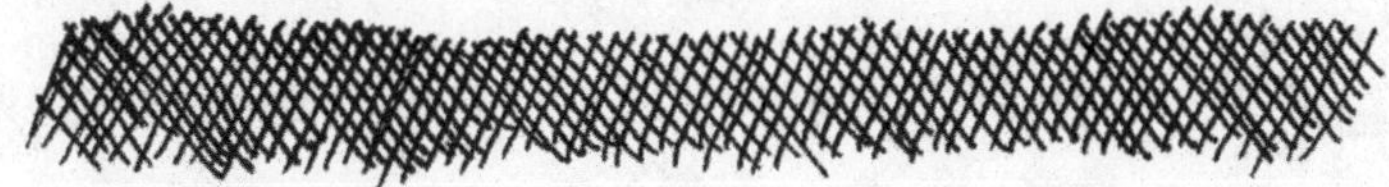

70

FORGET PARIS

Take the phrase "Forget (blank)," replace the blank with a word or phrase, make the new phrase the title of your poem, and then, write the poem. Possible titles include: "Forget This," "Forget About It," and "Forget Me Not." Don't forget to have fun with it.

71

HE SAID, SHE SAID

Write a poem with an interaction of some sort. The interaction does *not* have to be between people, though it can be. For instance, you could write about the interaction between a bee and a flower; or an owl and a field mouse. Or just write about a lawyer examining a witness. Just as long as there is some sort of interaction going on.

GOOD OLD DAYS

Write a "childhood" poem. This could be a poem about your own childhood or about someone else's.

POEMS ABOUT CHILDHOOD

Writing about childhood can cover a range of moods from deathly serious to whimsically silly. Plus, there are various entry points as evidenced by Shaindel Beers' *The Children's War and Other Poems*, which offers up several ekphrastic poems based on drawings by children who are in war zones. But there's also the charming "The Children's Hour" by Henry Wadsworth Longfellow, the silly "Constipation" by Ronald Wallace, and "The Raincoat," a bittersweet poem by Ada Limón.

73

WATERSHED MOMENTS

Write a "milestone" poem. It could be a work milestone, athletic milestone, or even a milestone related to diet or overcoming addiction.

74

NO TRICKS

Write a "treat" poem. This could be a trick or treat poem, or a poem about treating yourself (or another person) to something nice.

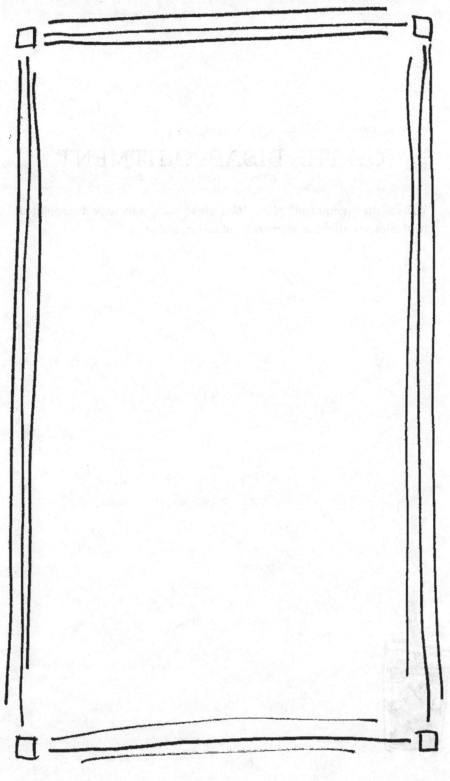

75

OH THE DISAPPOINTMENT

Write a "disappointment" poem. There are so many ways to be disappointed (with presents, affection, attention, motivation, and so on).

76

FOR THE TAKING

Write a "free" poem. Think free parking or a free space (in a board game). Think fat free, care free, or stone free (for all the Jimi Hendrix fans out there). Or think words with *free* in them, à la Freedom of Information Act.

77

EMPIRE STATE

Take the phrase "State of (blank)," replace the blank with a word or phrase, make the new phrase the title of your poem, and then write your poem. Possible titles include: "State of the Union," "State of Ohio," "State of Grace," or "State of Mind."

78

ON BEAUTY

Write a "beauty" poem. Think *Beauty and the Beast*; think beauty sleep; think airbrushed images in magazines, self-esteem, and selfies.

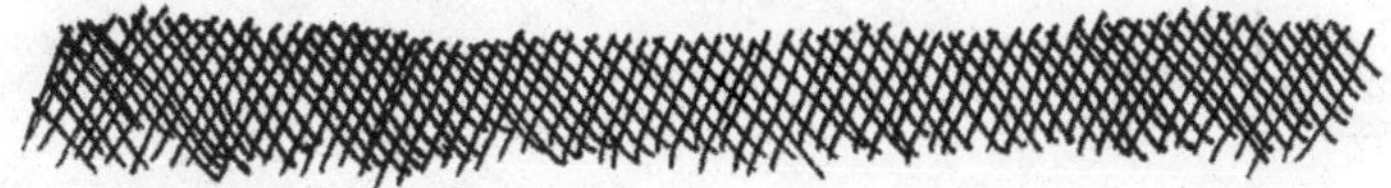

79

LIVING ON THE EDGE

Write an “excitement” poem. Excitement can be a good thing, but excitement can often lead to very bad things. So, whether your excitement leads to good results, bad results, or mixed results, I hope you’re excited to get poeming.

80

ENTHUSIAST POEM

Write a poem that incorporates a hobby (either yours or someone else's). That's right: Now is the perfect opportunity to write about your comic collection or your scrapbooking activities. Also, I think activities such as fishing, running, bowling, photography, birding, and gardening count as hobbies, too.

NEVER LOOK BACK

Write a poem of regret. Get creative with this one, but there should be some form of regret either expressed or hinted at (even if ever so slightly). You do *not* have to use the word "regret" in the poem, though it's fine if you do.

82

PICK UP LINES

Write a "pick up" poem. In the poem, you could write about picking stuff up—like operating a crane or cleaning a bedroom. Or it could be about picking up someone at a bar. Or picking up the pace. Or whatever else you happen to pick up … on.

ON LOVE POEMS

Love poems are about as controversial as you can get when talking to poets. Some folks love them, while others love to hate them. Maybe it's because they tend to produce abstract and flowery language (with rhymes like "love," "above," "blue," and "you" showing up frequently). But hey, there's a way around this: Dig into the details of the person of your affection. Pick a detail or two that is unique to your love.

83

BREAK IT DOWN

Write a "broken down" poem. Write about cars, lawn mowers, or the human spirit. So many possibilities for things and people to break down.

84

REMEMBER, REMEMBER

Take the phrase "Remember the (blank)," replace the blank with a word or phrase, make the new phrase the title of your poem, and then, write the poem. Of course, "Remember the Alamo" immediately springs to mind, but there are any number of things people can forget and need to remember. A few examples include: "Remember the Kids," "Remember the Dentist Appointment," and "Remember the One Time You Did That One Thing." Have fun remembering.

85

SCREEN TIME

Write a TV-inspired poem. It can be a poem about a game show, talk show, news show, or an entertaining series. The poem can be about commercials, remote controls, or having the biggest/best entertainment system in town. The poem can be about contemporary TV, or it can go old school. There are so many possibilities a poet could easily write a whole collection of poems based off this prompt.

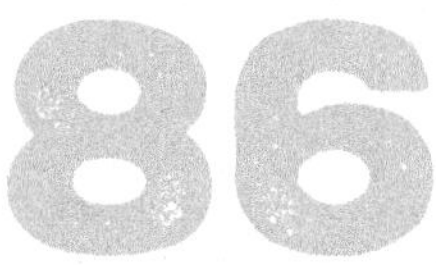

JUST MESSING AROUND

Write a "messing around" poem. There are a number of ways to take the phrase "messing around."

87

STOP THE PRESSES!

Write a "news" poem. There are the big headlines; there's the sports page, the comics, and the advertisements. There's always plenty happening in the world to prompt a poem.

CURRENT EVENT POEMS

The good thing about current events is that there's always something new to write about. The challenge is writing about a topic in a way that doesn't feel outdated five minutes after you've written it. One strategy I've seen successfully used by other poets is to take a big—almost abstract—story and make it personal and/or specific. In fact, that's a good trick for most poems.

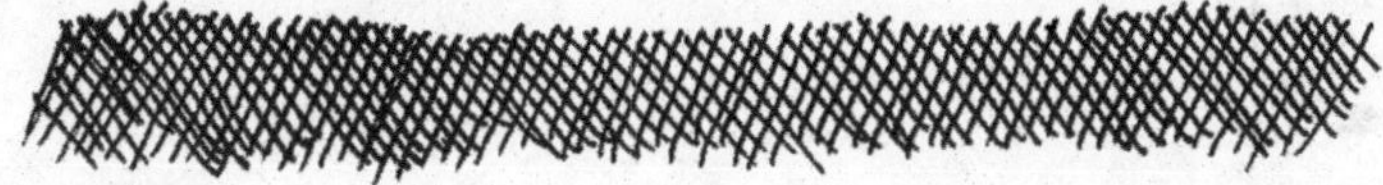

88

OUTSIDE THE LINES

Write an "outside" poem. Now, the poem itself can be about the great outdoors, but it can also be about other iterations of the outside concept. There's thinking outside the box, of course, but maybe just getting outside the cubicle or outside the bedroom, hospital room, depression, addiction, and our own heads.

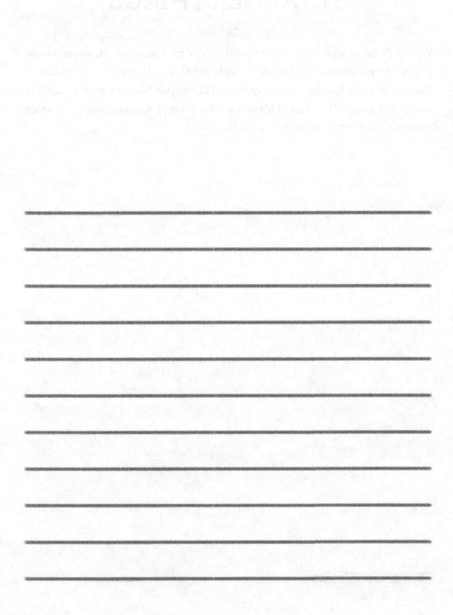

89

STRANGER THINGS

Write a poem in which you've imagined a story for a stranger. Maybe someone you see on public transportation, a couple at the laundromat, or a neighbor. Is the person more fabulous than expected? Fallen upon harder times? Exactly as one might guess? If you need ideas, use this prompt as an excuse to do some "research" by getting out and about in the world.

SURROUND YOURSELF

Write a "new surroundings" poem. The new digs could be a house, new work environment, the great outdoors, hotel room, etc. It can be exciting, sad, scary, and about any other emotion you can imagine.

91

ON HOLD

Take the phrase "Hold (blank)," replace the blank with a word or phrase, make the new phrase the title of your poem, and then, write your poem. Possible titles include: "Hold the Mayo," "Hold That Thought," or "Hold on a Minute." Anything you can or wish you could hold is fair game. Go hold something or someone—poetically speaking, of course.

92

INDUSTRIAL REVOLUTION

Write a poem of industry. Industry sounds like a big term, but it probably carries different connotations for different folks. For instance, some people might immediately think of the music industry (or mortgage industry), others may think of smokestacks, and some may think of industrious people they know or industrial-sized containers of food. Whatever industry means to you, try capturing (or conveying) it in a poem.

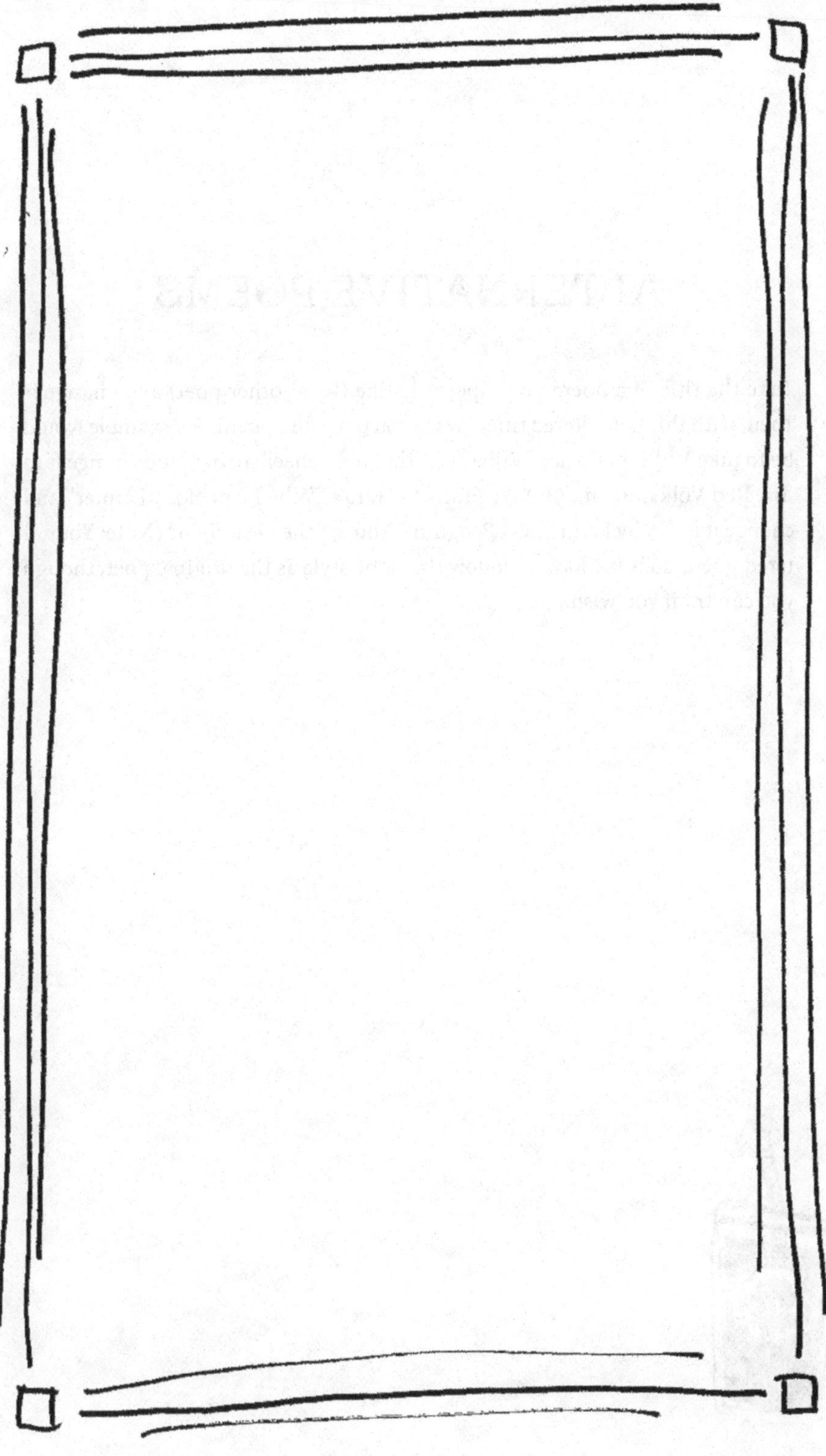

93

ALTERNATIVE POEMS

Take the title of a poem you especially like (by another poet) and change it. Then, with this new altered title, I want you to write a poem. An example would be to take William Carlos Williams' "The Red Wheelbarrow" and change it to "The Red Volkswagon." Or take Frank O'Hara's "Why I Am Not a Painter" and change it to "Why I Am Not a Penguin." You get the idea, right? (Note: Your altered poem does *not* have to follow the same style as the original poet, though you can try if you wish.)

94

PALM OF YOUR HAND

Write a "handheld" poem. Whether it's video games, smartphones, or soft tacos, the world is filled to the brim with things that can be held in one hand (or both).

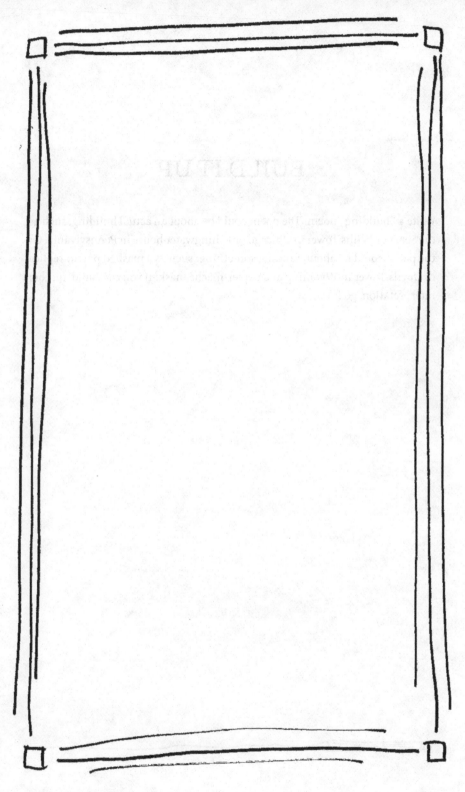

95

BUILD IT UP

Write a "building" poem. The poem could be about an actual building, such as the Sears or Willis Tower in Chicago or Fallingwater house in Pennsylvania. Or the poem could be about building something, such as a mashed potato replica of Devils Tower in Wyoming or a papier-mâché mask. If you can build another interpretation, go for it.

96

ANYWHERE BUT HERE

Write an "elsewhere" poem. Maybe elsewhere is a physical place—like Ohio instead of Georgia. Maybe elsewhere is a season—like summer instead of winter. Maybe elsewhere is a state of mind—like happy instead of depressed.

INTERESTED IN MORE POETIC FORMS?

I don't blame you if you are. I consider poetic forms fun poetry challenges. And the restrictions force me to take risks I wouldn't if I always let myself write free verse. Anyway, you can find a list of more than 80 poetic forms at the link www.writersdigest.com/whats-new/list-of-50-poetic-forms-for-poets.

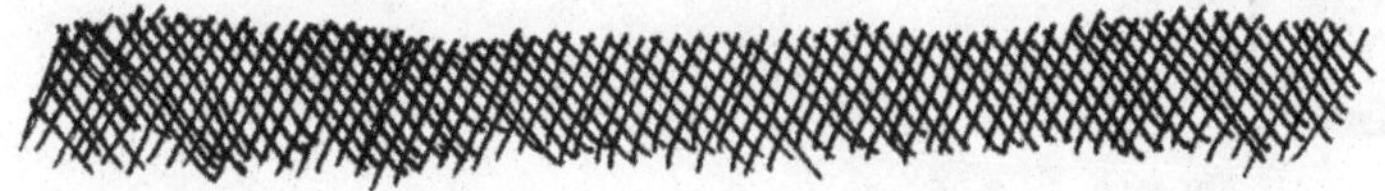

THAT'S WEIRD

Write a "weird" poem. Maybe it's a twist ending or a person on another planet (or another time). Maybe it's a land in which weird people are those that look just like us. Or whatever floats your boat.

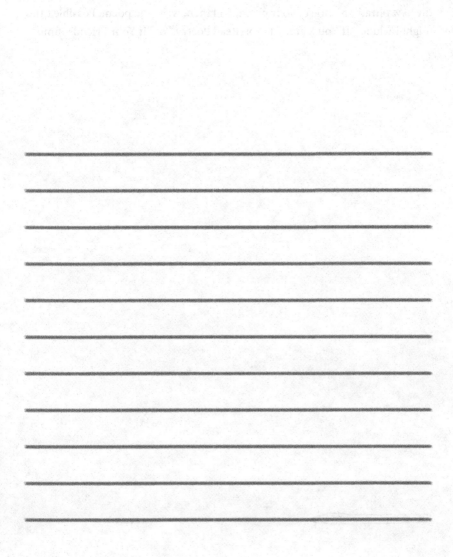

98

IF YOU GIVE A POET ...

Take the phrase "If You (blank)," replace the blank with a word or phrase, make the new phrase the title of your poem, and then, write the poem. Possible titles might include: "If You Dare," "If You Read Poetry," or "If Your Friends Jump."

THERE'S SOMETHING FISHY

Write a "fishy" poem. Perhaps the poem is about a fishy situation or action; perhaps the poem is about a fishy smell; or perhaps the poem is about an actual fish, whether fresh- or saltwater.

IDEAS FOR SHARING POEMS

After you've written so many poems, it's natural to want to share those poems with others. Some poets try to get their work published, but there are other ways to go about sharing your poems. When I was in high school, I would fill composition notebooks with poems and pass them around to friends, asking if they could put stars next to the poems they enjoyed. Of course, you can also share poems on blogs and social media profiles—like Facebook, Instagram, and even Twitter.

100

IT'S A CIRCUS IN HERE

Write a "circus" poem. It could be a three-ring circus, media circus, flea circus, or any other interpretation. It could be about people in the circus or those watching the circus. It could be about animals, clowns, tents, vendors, peanuts, etc.

101

ROAD TRIP

Write an "on the road" poem. It could be an "on the road again" poem à la Willie Nelson; or it could be a special new trip. Or an unexpected excursion—good or bad, day or night, etc.

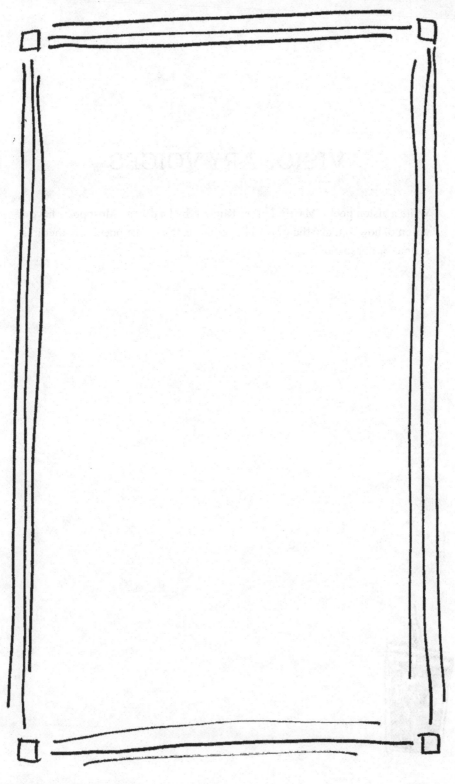

102

VISIONARY VOICES

Write a vision poem. Martin Luther King, Jr. had a dream. Most poets have a vision of how to make the world a better place. Write that poem, whether it is serious or not so much.

103

ROOM TO ROAM

Write a poem about something in the room (or space) you're sitting. The poem could be about a physical object in the room (or space). It could be a remembered or imagined event. If you're outside, then you've got plenty of possibilities.

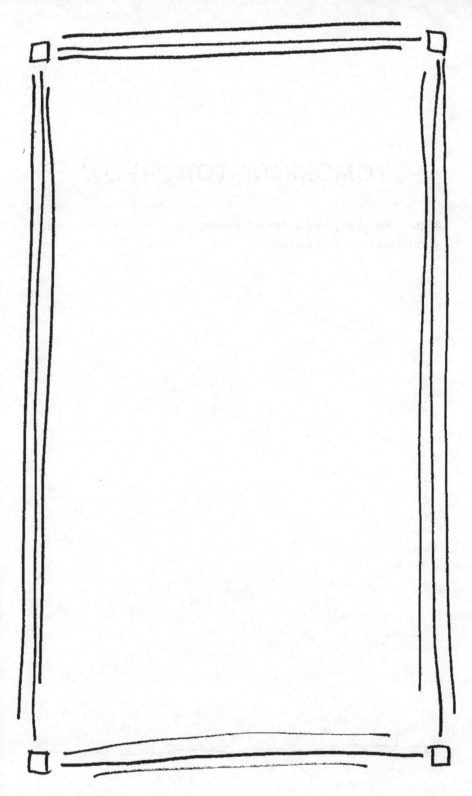

104

TOMORROW, TOMORROW

Write a "someday" poem. By "someday poem," I mean that you should write a poem about someday in the future.

105

HOLY

Take the phrase "Holy (blank)," replace the blank with a word or phrase, make the new phrase the title of your poem, and then, write your poem. Example titles might include "Holy Moly," "Holy Line Breaks," "Holy Jeans," and plenty of other more colorful variations. Feel free to replace the word "holy" with close approximations, such as "wholly" and "holey."

RELIGIOUS/SPIRITUAL POEMS

As with love poems, religious and spiritual poems run the risk of turning abstract and using overused rhymes. However, these poems pack quite a punch when done well. Here are a few examples that I like:

- "An Apology" by Kaveh Akbar
- "Psalm 150" by Jericho Brown
- "The Undeniable Pressure of Existence" by Patricia Fargnoli
- "Angels" by Nin Andrews
- "Ascension" by Joseph Mills

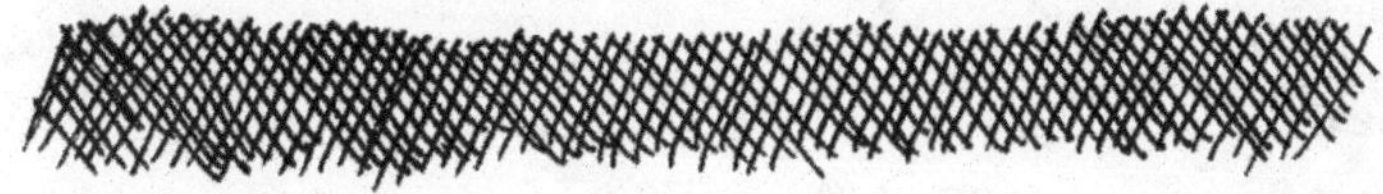

106

FOGGY BOTTOM

Write a "fog" poem. The poem can be about a fog. It can incorporate a fog. Or it can delve into concepts like the "fog of war" or "foggy intentions."

107

MISTAKES HAVE BEEN MADE

Write a "mistake" poem. The poem itself could be a mistake, if you want to go that route, but it could also be a case of mistaken identity, a clerical error, or some other mishap. The narrator of the poem could be sorry for making the mistake or upset that someone else made one.

108

FULLY CHARGED

Write a "charged" poem. Maybe the poem has an electrical charge or a charge to a credit card. Or maybe there's a charge from a bull or a battle charge. There are any number of ways to charge the old poetic battery with this prompt.

109

OLD VERSE

Write an "old" poem. The poem could be about an older individual, or an older way of thinking.

110

MAGICAL MOMENT

Write a "magic" poem. The world is filled with magic for those who are open to seeing it. Sure, some of it's trickery and sleight of hand, but there's also a magic to everyday moments and situations, certain notes in favorite songs, even mistakes that end up being so perfect artists can only claim magic. I hope you can conjure up a bit of magic with this prompt.

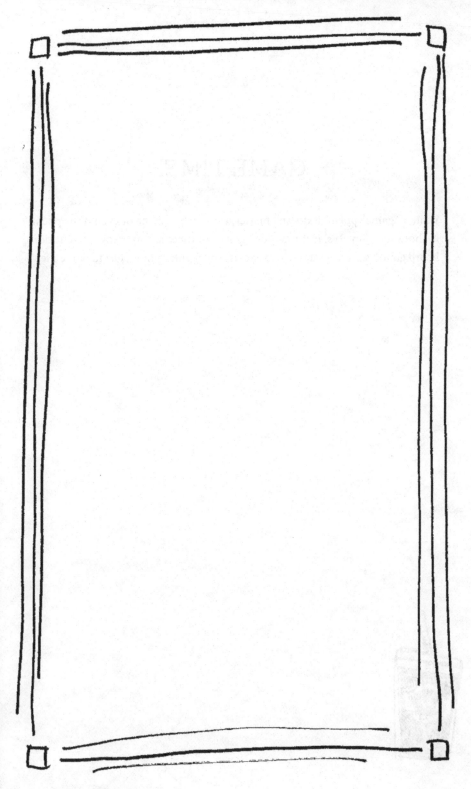

111

GAME TIME

Write a "game" poem. It doesn't matter what type of game or even if the poem is about the game (vs. just mentioning it), but there are so many possibilities: board games, sports games, video games, and mental games, just to name a few.

POETRY GAMES

Poetry is a solitary act, right? Well, yeah … except when it isn't. There are actually collaborative party games available to poets. For instance, renga is a Japanese poetic game in which the first poet writes three lines (a hokku or haiku) and the next poet writes two lines (seven syllables each). Two or more poets follow this pattern for as long as they wish. Another poetic game is called exquisite corpse in which one person writes a line or two, folds a piece of paper so only part of the writing shows, and passes it to the next writer. It's a game developed by the surrealists and is still played today.

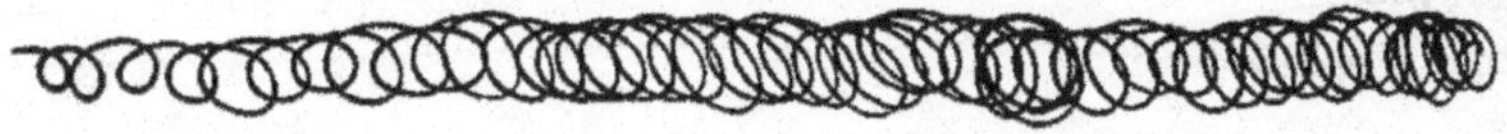

112

LEARNING CURVE

Take the phrase "Learning (blank)," replace the blank with a word or phrase, make the new phrase the title of your poem, and then, write your poem. Possible titles might include: "Learning to Love," "Learning to Forget," "Learning More Than I Ever Thought I'd Need to Know About Eggplants," and so many other possible topics to learn.

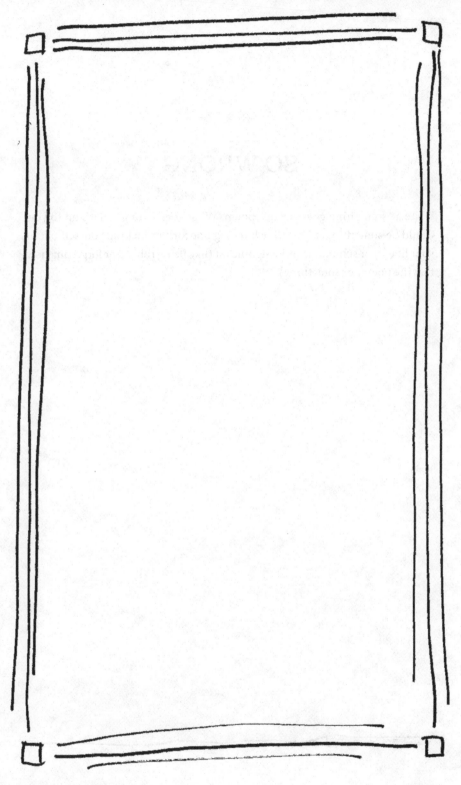

113

SO WRONG

Write a “something goes wrong” poem. What goes wrong? That’s up to you. Could be something minor (like burning popcorn or locking yourself out of your house) or something more significant (like being robbed or forgetting how to write poetry or something).

114

DAILY SPECIAL

Write a "special day" poem. A special day could be a holiday, birthday, anniversary, or just a day when everything changed. There are special days that everyone recognizes and special days that maybe only you (or a small group of folks) appreciate. If it's special to you, then it's fair game for this prompt.

115

EX POST FACTO

Write an "ex" poem. Of course, writing about an ex-spouse or ex-job are fair game, but any words that start with "ex" should be good, too. You don't have to explain or extend an exacting explanation of how you decide to expand upon this explosive prompt; I'm sure exotic examples are extraneous.

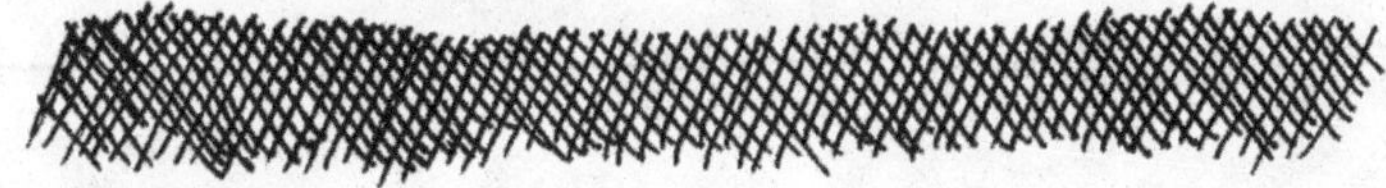

116

TWO WEEKS' NOTICE

Write a "notice" poem. A notice could be a warning about something. Or it could just be an informational type of notice. Or perhaps, you just noticed a person, place or thing for the first time.

117

GENERATOR

Write a "generation" poem. A generation poem could be about the generation-X or the baby boomers, sure, but it could also be about generating poems and/or power. Or regeneration of limbs. Or any number of other topics you wish to generate.

118

INTELLIGENCE FACTOR

Write an "intelligence" poem. Of course, intelligence is subjective. What is common sense for one person makes no sense to another. But intelligence is more than IQ and test scores. There's artificial intelligence, intelligent animals, and military intel. And I've found that many poets have a special intelligence of their own.

119

MAKING WAVES

Take the phrase "(blank) wave," replace the blank with a word or phrase, make the new phrase the title of your poem, and then, write your poem. Possible titles include: "Tidal Wave," "Next Wave," "Friendly Wave," "Heat Wave," and/or "Sound Wave."

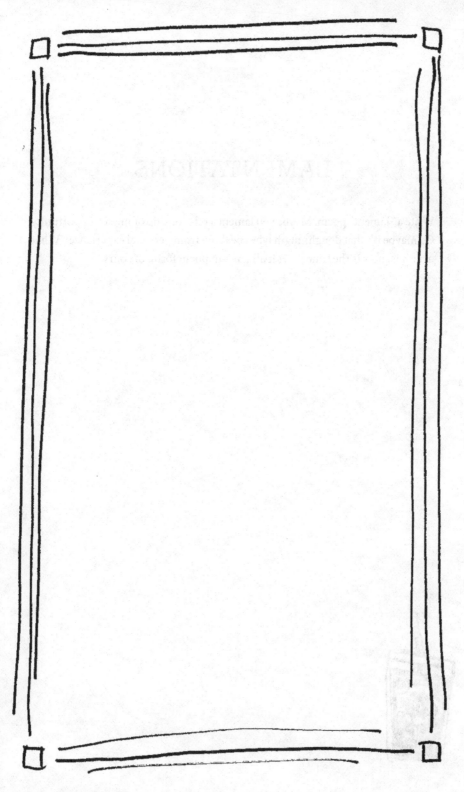

120

LAMENTATIONS

Write a "lament" poem. Maybe you lament a relationship or missed opportunity. Or maybe it's that doughnut (maybe speaking from personal experience). Whatever it is, now is the time to let it all out—in poem form, of course.

121

PLAYING FAVORITES

Write a "favorite" poem. Maybe that sounds a bit silly, but what I mean is to write a poem about something that's your favorite. A favorite teacher. Favorite movie. Favorite ice cream flavor. I don't know, because I have my own list of favorites. Only you can do you ... and your favorites. Who knows? Maybe this will end up being your favorite prompt.

122

MOMENT OF INTRIGUE

Pick an intriguing and/or seldom-used word, make it the title of your poem, and then, write your poem. If you have a limited vocabulary, try out *brabble*, *dandle*, *feracious*, *impavid*, *lippitude*, or *vulgus*. Or pick up a dictionary or thesaurus.

NEED A FEW MORE IDEAS?

Here are a few more words to consider:

- Aglet—that plastic tube at the end of your shoelaces
- Jalopy—an old vehicle
- Mortadella—a large smoked sausage seasoned with pepper and garlic
- Pettifogger—a person who quibbles over trifles
- Roustabout—an unskilled worker
- Tampion—a plug or cover for the muzzle of a gun

123

FOODIE

Pick a food, make it the title of your poem, and write your poem. It can be a food you love, a food you hate, or food you've never even tried before. Your poem can be about the food—or not. Your choice.

124

NO RESERVATIONS

Write a "reserved" poem. A table or room can be reserved. A person can be reserved in their speech or mannerisms. I give full permission for poets to reserve the right to write without reservation.

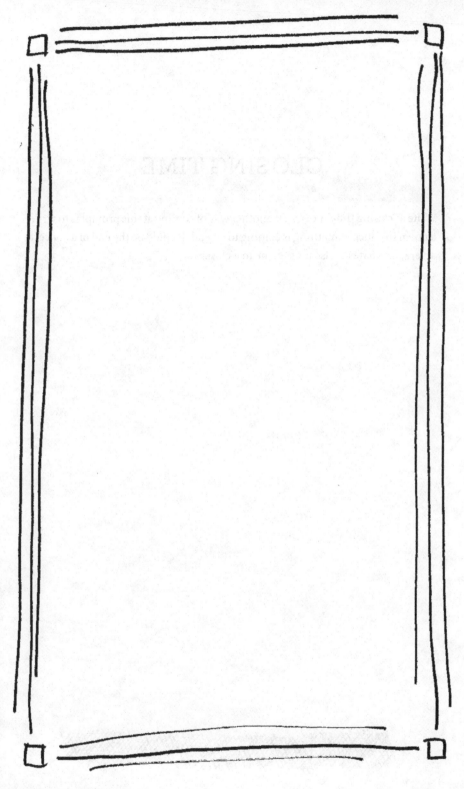

125

CLOSING TIME

Write a "closing time" poem. Or another way of coming at this prompt is to write a poem in which something is coming to an end. It could be the end of a concert, an era, or whatever else must come to a close.

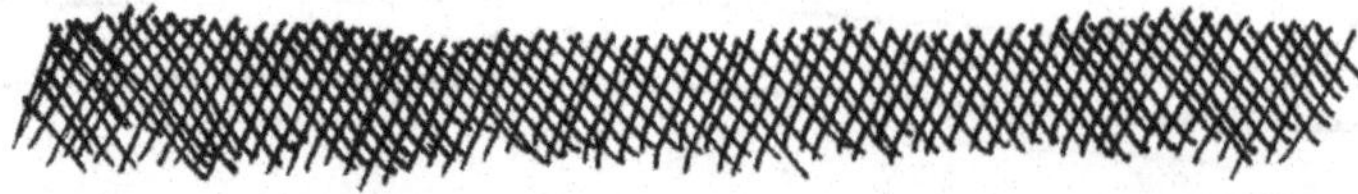

PARTING WORDS AND RESOURCES

If you just finished writing a poem for every prompt, then wow! Great job! If you haven't even started yet because you like to flip to the back first, I totally feel you and tend to do that myself. Now, get writing!

Back to the finishers: I hope that was as fun for you as it's been for me over the years. Hopefully, you've learned more about what works for you and your writing process—and maybe even learned a few new things about poetry in those occasional sidebars scattered throughout the book. Let's keep it going!

For the poems you've already written, consider revising and/or recreating them with fresh eyes. What works best for me is to pretend that someone else wrote them, which allows me to be a little more objective when looking over my own words.

After you feel they're the best they can be, consider trying to get them published in print and online magazines and journals. I happen to edit a great resource that includes submission guidelines for hundreds of poetry publishing opportunities; it's called *Poet's Market*. Check it out.

Also, keep writing! If you need new prompts, no problem. Go to the Writers Digest.com website and check out the Poetic Asides blog. Most of the prompts in this book started on the blog in some form or another. We poem every day in the months of April and November, as well as on Wednesdays the rest of the year. All are welcome.

Until next we meet, keep poeming!
Robert Lee Brewer
www.writersdigest.com/editor-blogs/poetic-asides

ABOUT THE AUTHOR

Robert Lee Brewer is the author of *Solving the World's Problems* (Press 53) and the *Writer's Digest Guide to Poetic Forms*. For more than a decade, he's edited the annual *Writer's Market* and *Poet's Market* books and recently took over *Guide to Literary Agents*. He maintains the Poetic Asides blog on WritersDigest.com and writes the Poetic Asides column for *Writer's Digest* magazine. In other words, he has an awesome job that also involves programming online writing conferences, speaking nationally at writing and publishing events, judging writing contests, and more. And he's a former Poet Laureate of the Blogosphere and one of the few poets on the planet to be name-dropped in both *O, The Oprah Magazine* and *Poetry* magazine.

Beyond all those professional shenanigans, he's married to the poet Tammy Foster Brewer, who helps him chase around their five amazing kids. He used to call them his little poets, but more than half of them are teenagers now and nearly as tall as he is and would prefer he write bestselling novels instead of poetry. Time flies.

He shows up here and there on social media—and can usually be found with a public profile as "Robert Lee Brewer." For instance, you can follow him on Twitter @RobertLeeBrewer and on Instagram at www.instagram.com/robertleebrewer.

Printed in the United States
by Baker & Taylor Publisher Services